How to Analyze People

Proven Techniques for Reading Body Language & Identifying Personality Types and Dark Psychology

Additionally, the information in the following pages is intended only for informational purposes and should thus be thought of as universal. As befitting its nature, it is presented without assurance regarding its prolonged validity or interim quality. Trademarks that are mentioned are done without written consent and can in no way be considered an endorsement from the trademark holder.

Table of Contents

Introduction

Thank you for downloading *How to Analyze People: Proven Techniques for Reading Body Language & Identifying Personality Types and Dark Psychology.*

What is body language? Well, it is as it sounds. When we speak to someone and simply interact with them, they give off "cues" that are a type of non-verbal language. Everyone one of us does this, in fact. It is ingrained in each of us. I certainly know I do. Reading someone else's body language is not the same as reading their mind, and yet there are so many universal clues, so many ways people "behave" with their bodies that are indisputably meant to signify one thing. The two abilities almost rank up there side-to-side—that is if you have done your homework and you know what you are doing when it comes to reading body language.

There are things to keep in mind when we attempt to read someone by their body language. Number one is that it is, in fact, we are attempting to read their mind. Everything that we do, every little gesture our hands make—the direction in which our eyes are facing, all of this—is wired into us through our brains. So in effect, if you are reading someone's body language you might as well be reading his or her mind.

This brings up an interesting question about ethics. Would you read someone's mind if you could? I would not, except in situations where I or someone I love could potentially be in danger. I believe that what goes on privately in someone's mind is just that—private.

However, body language is slightly different. I believe it is there to be read. I also believe we can save ourselves time (and potentially grief) if we learn to read it and read it well.

In this book, you will learn many of the very basic body language cues and maybe a few not so basic ones. It is up to you to use them to your advantage. First, you must learn to trust them, and this can only come from a bit of trial and error. That is okay. Life itself is a big long experiment in trial and error.

I believe that simply by having a good grasp on body language, we can learn so much about a person that we could save ourselves a potential heartache down the road. We can come to understand what types of people we would like to be friends with and the ones we do not.

You can learn later on whether someone has our back or if they do not. This is huge. Knowing whom you can trust can make all of the difference in life, and believe me: we all have to have at least a few people that we can trust unequivocally. In fact, so much about life itself is trust. Therefore, if you are not a Witch Doctor or a psychic, reading this book will get you as close as you need to be to "read" another person. Pay close attention and enjoy!

Chapter 1:

An Introduction to Body Language

"As the tongues speaketh to the ear so the gesture speaketh the eye."

—Francis Bacon

The actual name for body language is "kinesics." The study of body language is not an ancient one. Relatively, in fact, it hasn't been around that long. The most serious interest in the field has just come about in the 20th Century. The 60s and 70s are when studies in this area really started to take off. *How to a Read a Person Like a Book* published in 1979, by Gerald Nierenberg, is often credited for piquing interest in many folks who had not considered the concept before. The science of being able to read body is fascinating and unique, and there has been much invaluable information developed and learned through the study of it.

Having an idea about how to read body language has definitely given us an advantage because reading body language is the closest thing we have to read minds. I have seen too much in my life to discount that the possibility for one person to read another's mind does not exist entirely, but it has yet to be proven in any sort of scientific way.

You can gain a plethora of information about a person simply from using their body language. You can learn things about their personality, and perhaps more importantly, their intentions. There are many good reasons to study body language. If you're in that (what can seem like for some of us) perpetual cycle of the dating game and would like to find someone fitted for you, body language is a perfect tool for you.

Many of us have gone through bad relationships, nasty break-ups, or divorces. Some of us try again and some of us just figure that we are better off alone. There is certainly nothing wrong with that. Being single and living alone is not without merit. Many adults who reside alone know that there are small luxuries that come with it that can easily be overlooked—things as simple as stretching out in your own bed at night. Perhaps you like to surround yourself with important possessions like books, journals, your computer, and your phone. Maybe even a dog or a cat or two. It is hard to have room for all of these things and one more person as well.

When you live alone, it is at your sole discretion what time the lamp is turned off, the television, or the music. You get to eat what you like for meals whenever you like to eat them. Dinner and a glass of wine in bed with a movie at 3:00 p.m. on a Sunday afternoon—who's to stop you?

There's a bright side to everything and being half of a couple isn't for everyone, and yet as a society, we tend to emphasize "coupling up." Those who are single are sometimes viewed as unfortunate. Not everyone realizes some people are that way by choice. Instead, they tend to feel sorry for people who choose to stay single, not taking in to account all of the circumstances. It has been ingrained in our minds for a million years; people are meant to pair up.

Regardless of, I suppose, having strayed a little off-point there, the main point I was trying to make is that it's probably in romantic scenarios that body language gets used the most. It is very important. It could save you a lot of grief down the road, and who has time for grief?

9

Then, of course, there are virtually endless other types of relationships that exist. What about friends, in general? As we become adults, it has been my experience that most of us learn that making friends is just a little harder (at least) than when we were little or very young. As children, things seem to come about more easily. When a child meets another on the playground, at a certain age, it can easily happen that they end up becoming "best friends" practically overnight. In fact, many of us have friends dating back that far. I have a girlfriend I met when I was seven. We were neighbors. Her father had an old VW Van parked in his yard and we used to spend endless hours inside "road-tripping." Oh, what would I give to have that childlike imagination back! We remained friends throughout our school years and while geographically our lives took us in a different direction, we often find ourselves having late night conversations about life via Facebook Messenger. She's a treasure. It was not an attraction that took place based on body language. It just happened. Life is simpler in general when you are a child.

As we grow up, we are told to choose our friends wisely, for our friends are ultimately a reflection of ourselves. However, how do we do that—the choosing wisely part? It is much more daunting (or can be too many people) than it looks to be on paper. We meet people and we either feel drawn to them or not. We have no way of knowing what kind of person they are right off the bat—or do we?

Having said all that, there exist a plethora of other reasons to read body language than for the benefit of strictly romantic or even friendship reasons.

Examine how many different kinds of relationships we have. Think, for a moment about the nature of those relationships. Besides our spouses or significant others, boyfriends/

girlfriends, etc., there are our children, our parents. There are also co-workers, friends, acquaintances, in-laws; this list could really go on.

We don't have to "read" everyone. When I drop off my dry-cleaning and pick it up a few days later, it pretty much makes no difference to me as to what the person who cleaned my clothes is like, as long as they did a good job, and of course it's always a bonus of the people we interact with regularly are "nice," in general.

However, if I am single and I am considering someone to date or my friend is in the same boat and she has someone in mind, you can bet that those are people I want to "read" as much as I can.

My boss is another person I want to be able to read. By having this ability, it automatically gives me a "leg-up" on the competition. In addition, it gives me invaluable clues to what he thinks of me, which could ultimately end up affecting my bottom dollar. By learning to "read" him, I believe I saved myself a lot of stress. I can be easily intimidated at times, and when my boss walks into a board meeting looking like he is in a terrible mood, I was the first one to wonder if that mood had anything directly to do with me. It helped me study his body language; learn his "tics." As it turns out, I was never the cause of his stress. No surprises there, as I, and people in general, tend to overthink in those types of situations.

It is perfectly normal too—not only wanting to get to know someone but to know what that person thinks of *you* as well. Some people's body language is harder to read. For instance, I have learned that some can lie much better than others can. There have been people in my life who have lied to me and I knew it the second the words came out of their mouth. In truth, some people are *terrible* liars. Most people put out the classic signals and more, such as a kind of nervousness and sense of guilt. However, there are people who lie like a rug—as the expression goes—and no one would be the wiser. For my own sanity, I choose to believe there are more good people in the world than there are otherwise. If a person can pull off a lie, not give off any of the signals, and act cool as a cucumber, I would certainly be leery. If, on the other hand, someone tried to lie to me and did a terrible job of it, I would not automatically discount that person for having to try to lie. I would try to understand the reason and not necessarily judge them for it.

People have their reasons. That is another thing I have come to understand. Sometimes people seem "aloof" and "stuck-up" when what they really are is painfully shy. I consider it my mission that if someone were that shy, I would reach out to him or her if I could. I was terribly shy as a child and teenager so I know the feeling. It's truly mortifying in certain circumstances.

Thanks to a collection of very subtle and not-so-subtle cues that every human being gives off in their interactions with others, it decidedly is possible to know much more about a person than you might think.

Chapter 2:

Classic Body Language Signs

Are you a person who enjoys "people-watching?" Many do. Some people enjoy it so much they can simply get lost for long periods, sitting on a bench in a mall, or lingering over a cup of coffee in a restaurant for the sole purpose of observing those around them.

People are constantly giving cues about what's going on inside their minds and as a natural process; these cues translate to movements or gestures of the body. Some can be very subtle, while others not so much. Have you ever noticed a group of folks talking to one another in a circle? Next time you do, just for fun, take a close look at how each one is presenting themselves.

One person might be leaning in towards the middle of the pack. Another might be standing a foot back with their arms folded. Standing with arms folded is a well-known sign that, for one reason or another, that person is feeling somewhat closed-off or defensive. For some reason, he or she is establishing a slight distance between the people with whom they happen to be interacting. If you are not attuned to such things, it might not be something you notice right off the bat.

If you work at an office, next time you stop to chat for a few moments with a co-worker in the break room, watch what they do with their body as you carry on your conversation. What is the positioning of their arms? Are they folded? Opened and at their side? In their pockets, perhaps? Here are some basic body gestures for you to watch for in all manner of situations.

1. Is a person facing you square on or are they turned slightly away? Are they even looking at you while you speak to them or does their attention remain concentrated on the cup of coffee or tea they might be preparing? If they are not squarely facing you or have their backs turned to you, they are most likely not interested in what you have to say.

2. Assuming they are facing you, are they looking into your eyes as you speak? Is their gaze steady? Eye contact is huge. A person needs to have the ability to look you in the eye. If they don't, something isn't right.

3. Imagine you are having a conversation in the break room at work. Let us imagine the other party is facing you. How is their posture, the position of their shoulders? Are their backs straight and their shoulders squared? Generally, this is a sign of confidence and an "ease in one's own skin." This is usually perceived as a positive body language stance. It relates to you due to the fact that they clearly feel confident and at ease with you.

4. Let's say you are taking to the same person and put things into a different light. Let's say this person's shoulders are "curled" or "hunched." This is actually a sign that the person you are speaking to is feeling a slight need to "protect themselves" in some way. They can be signaling feelings of vulnerability or insecurity. Keep in mind that this does not necessarily mean that this person feels vulnerable with you or even insecure speaking to you. It is a more subtle clue and there could be many reasons for it.

When you are not sure, yet you're talking to this person, and their shoulders are curled inward, how would you know if it's you or if it's simply the way that person carries themselves fairly constantly based on their internal view of life and their confidence—or lack thereof—in themselves? Fortunately, there is a simple answer. You look for other cues. Sometimes a certain body language trait is nothing more than a one-off. Perhaps that person's shoulders are rounded because they are simply very physically tired. Possibly, they even suffered a bout of scoliosis early in life. Maybe they were unable to sleep the night before and it feels physically taxing to stand in their normal stance. Many times, however, one piece of body language can be just one piece out of many, and when you put your pieces together, sort of like a puzzle, you can see the picture much more clearly.

Self-confidence throughout our lives is hugely variable from person to person. People make their way through lives armed with widely varying degrees of self-confidence throughout all different types of situations. This can be due to how they were raised and what they learned growing up. If while growing up, it is constantly communicated to you that you are worthwhile and good and you grow up in a positive, nurturing environment, it is likely that you will have a good deal of natural self-confidence.

On the contrary, people grow up in all sorts of sad, abusive, and otherwise less-than-ideal circumstances. There are people who are simply lacking confidence in themselves. In some people, this deeply inherent trait will not change without counseling or education and practice or some recognition and applied effort on their part.

5. As you are speaking, does your colleague maintain eye contact and continue to face you? Alternatively, do they perhaps turn their back on you slightly and begin a task? If they do this, it could mean that they are not actually that interested in what you have to say. It is, to say the least, dismissive. This can easily leave you feeling like you are being condescended to. People appear not to realize it since it has almost become normal in so many cases, but looking down at one's smartphone and scrolling through the messages or missed calls is not only simply demonstrative that you have poor social skills, it indicates that you have very little interest in hearing what the other person has to say. If this becomes the case during a conversation, it is not a positive body language.

6. How is this person stance during your conversation? Have they stood there easily, or do they shift their weight back and forth often? Have their feet been moving as if they're practicing a dance step? If so, this indicates that they're uncomfortable. Therefore, maybe you do, after all, intimidate this person and make them feel slightly ill at ease. But hey, take heart. Those same movements can also indicate impatience, and that could mean absolutely nothing to do with you. It could be that they are in the middle of a big project and they really need to get back to their desk, so say it's not you but rather an actual nervousness or an impatient feeling that, while they may be enjoying their time with you, they really do need to be getting back. Keep in mind, another reason a person might feel ill at ease with you, in the beginning, is because they find themselves attracted to you. It's in an exhibition of shyness, in a sense.

7. As you talk to him, does he softly stroke his face? If he does it might seem cheesy, but it really isn't. This is a sign that he's really hearing what you're saying. He would like to stroke YOUR face but he doesn't dare, or you two aren't intimate enough for that to be appropriate. This is a good sign—a sweet sign. Making a true effort to listen to someone shows that he cares about you.

8. Do his actions show that he is protective of you? You know how when you are walking, maybe wearing heels, and a guy will lightly place his hand on your back as a sort of protective gesture. This is a way of saying, "I've got your back" through body language.

As you can see from just this one short chapter, there is so much to reading body language. Not only is it up to you to pick up on the verbal clues, with many of them you must decide exactly which way to interpret these clues because it just happens that sometimes there are more ways than one. When reading body language, it's up to you to put all of the clues together before you make any definitive decisions.

Body language is an indicator of many things. Is someone attracted to you? Is someone the opposite of being attracted? Are they stressed? Angry? Sad? What about their self-esteem? Is it high? Low? Are they overly confident even when they don't seemingly have any reason to be?

Then there's the darker side of things. Are there ways to tell if a human being is inherently bad through their body language, gestures, eye contact or lack thereof, etc.? The answer is a resounding yes.

Chapter 3:

Portraying Confidence

Was your mother always telling you to sit up straight? Mine did. Besides the fact that it's better for your body overall and the health of your back, in particular, you simply project a better image when you sit up straight. Slouching is not an attractive look.

Don't hunker. Particularly, don't hunker over your phone. Few things make you appear more vulnerable than being hunched over your phone.

Cellphones are wonderful tools, but the problem is when we are absorbed in them, we are not projecting strength and confidence. When you go out, look around you. People wait everywhere: waiting rooms for doctors, lines in the grocery store, lines to pick up prescriptions, and people waiting to get haircuts. You will see these people curled up and exhibiting bad posture, with their entire attention sucked into their electronic device. Of course, it's necessary to use your phone, but if you are trying to present yourself in an attractive way, put it in your pocket for a bit. Far from projecting confidence and power, being on our phones in public give the impression that we are not as aware as our surrounds as we should be. That's not an attractive trait.

Smile

Walking around with a smile on your face all the time certainly beats a frown. However, smiling too much can make you appear submissive. Again, you want to project confidence. You want people to see that you are strong. I'm not saying you should go around frowning. Having a pleasant and approachable look on your face is good, but save the big, genuine smile for when it is truly warranted.

Be "Big"

Stand up tall and take up as much space around you as you can (without casually sprawling out when inappropriate.) By doing this, not only are you projecting confidence to others, you are also investing in your own self-confidence. You know the old saying, "Walk in there like you own the place?" Do that. Walk around like you own the place and watch what it does for your own self-confidence.

Meet People's Eyes

Eye contact has long been a reliable predictor of someone's general personality. Think about the last person you met that was unable to look you in the eye and think of how uneasy that made you. It causes a person to think, "Something isn't right about this person."

When you are introduced to people when you are ordering coffee, sitting in a job interview, meet people directly in the eye with a steady unwavering gaze. I'm not saying stare them down and ultimately make them uncomfortable, simply look them in the eye.

Besides, you are going to want to do that anyway so that you can get a handle on what kind of person you're dealing with. There's something not quite right about a person who cannot look you directly in the eye.

If you are shy, and this is difficult for you, practice in the mirror or with a trusted friend. This one is very important.

Be an Excellent Listener

Do you know those people who turn away and fidget a lot when you are trying to talk to them? Never be one of them. When someone is talking to you, put all of you into the act of listening. Keep your eyes on their eyes and their face, face them, and don't let yourself be distracted by anything else.

Listening to someone makes him or her feel valued in a way that few things can. Make sure to listen to what they are saying as well. Don't ever just sit and "wait" for your turn to talk. Don't formulate your answer when they are talking. You listen until they are finished talking. Then, if you need a moment or two to consider what they've said and formulate your response, that's fine. Perfect listening skills are priceless. It makes you look good and there's no better way to get to know another person as well as listening carefully to the things they say and taking in their demeanor as they say them.

Watch the Inflection in your Voice

Have you ever noticed how some people seem to put a question mark at the end of almost every statement? So, you know what I mean? No matter what they say, it's a question?

This makes people seem less intelligent, less decisive, and less together. Pay attention to the intonation and inflection when you speak. Only raise your voice at the end of actual questions. You might have to watch this one for a while. Pay particular attention because if you do it, you might not even be aware that you do. It's worth it though. It makes a world of difference.

Hand Gestures

You can portray yourself as confident using hand gestures or you can portray yourself as mousy. With your hands, you can even come off a little crazy.

Some people really don't use hand gestures when they speak, or at least they don't "talk with their hands," per se. Non-gesticulations are sometimes perceived as somewhat lackluster or indifferent when they speak. Some people are very animated and use their hands all over their place to emphasize their speech. People who "talk" with their hands are perceived as being slightly more intelligent than those who do not.

The one thing you definitely don't want to do when you speak is hide your hands. This sends out an unconscious perception to the listener that perhaps you have something to hide.

According to an article in _Psychology Today_, the following hand gestures are perceived to indicate the following:

- Hands open and palms at a 45-degree angle: This is thought to communicate that you are being honest and open.

- Hand open and palms down: Think of the expression "hands down." As in, "I'm telling you—she was hands-down the prettiest girl in the room."

- Palms facing each other with fingers together: Conveys you are in full possession of expertise in whatever it is you are discussing. This is good to know!

- Hands grasped in front of you: You're nervous! You want to avoid this one at all costs in order to come across as confident at as you can.

- Hand gestures larger than your body outline: This one can mean two things.

1. The idea you are trying to communicate is bigger than you are.

2. You are coming off as being chaotic. Be careful with this one.

There's actually an interesting dynamic behind the phenomena of "speaking with your hands." If you do it and you find yourself embarrassed by it, you really shouldn't be. According to studies, using your hands when you speak is a powerful aid in helping you get your point across, not to mention people who use their hands while speaking are considered more intelligent.

In a study that was conducted analyzing TED Talks, it was discovered that the speakers perceived to be the most dynamic and attractive used 465 hand gestures on average. Keep in mind, this number equates to almost twice as much as the least popular speakers studied. There have been many other studies conducted as well and it's been discovered that people who gesticulate the most while speaking are looked at as people who are more warm and agreeable. Conversely, the opposite is true for those who did not use hand gestures when they spoke.

Knowing that, some hand gestures can be viewed as "over the top." You certainly don't want to appear as though you are simultaneously speaking and practicing karate.

Studies have turned up some interesting facts about hand gestures. Using hand gestures is a way to place emphasis on the most crucial points you are attempting to make.

Someone watching you speak might not fully grasp the importance of your point, yet they will know that you are making a very important point, thus giving them food for thought for after your speech. It's there for them to take in visually and not just audibly. This has everything to do with the emotion and the passion behind what you are communicating to your audience. Gesturing is kind of like a second form of speech, in this manner. It's very powerful and backing up your words.

Chapter 4:

On the Darker Side

This book deals with both light and dark signs of body language. The point of the book is for you to be on alert for what to watch out for when dealing with other people. Dark Psychology is all too abundant in the people around us. We'd like to think that everyone is "light" and "good." Sadly, however, that is not the case. However, by knowing exactly what to be on alert for, you're already a step ahead. We all have friends, lovers, and family. Those people look out for us in the best way they can. However, can they always be there looking out for us? No. That's why it's part of our personal responsibility to be able to read other people to a certain degree. Our number one goal should be to look out for ourselves and keep ourselves safe from those unpleasant people who unfortunately exist in the world.

I'll list some traits and some body language signals for you to educate yourself. I am an optimist, and I do believe more good than bad exists in the world, and yet, it's certainly our duty to know how to read which is which.

Revisit this scenario with me. Picture this. You're single. You're on the lookout for a possible opportunity to go out with someone. You meet a guy. Right of the bat, you notice he's a looker. He's exactly your type. For fun, let's just say he's tall, a bit lanky, and fit-dressed in designer jeans. His hair is dark, of medium length, and neither too "styled" nor too messy. His eyes are a piercing blue. He has everything you like in a man,

23

aesthetically. On top of it all, he looks to be right about your age. Score!

As you talk, you notice that he's saying all the right words. This is looking good. However, there are certain cues that should not be overlooked. He's expressing things with his words, yet does his body language match his words? That's what you will always need to be on the lookout for. The old saying "actions speak louder than words" applies to body language as well. In fact, it could have been written for body language alone. Therefore, here are the things you need to look out for. Body language sends a powerful message. You are about to learn how to decode it. The following are signs people give off with their body language. I'm including both the good and the bad.

Licking His Lips

This one may seem odd—somewhat cheesy as if you're watching a bad 1970s rom-com. Yet, it has long been proven that when an animal is eyeing something he badly wants, he'll lick his lips in anticipation. Although this one might seem outdated somehow, it isn't. It's coded in our genes. Here's a not so subtle example. When a waiter sets a delectable looking desert down in front of you at the dinner table, do you lick your lips at least once before taking the first bite? I'd be willing to bet you do.

This gesture is open to interpretation and is not always definitively "light" or "dark." A man can lick his lips in a kind of predatory gesture. It's up to you to pair it up with the other signs to determine what this one means.

Raising an Eyebrow

Does he raise one eyebrow quickly? Pay attention to how he does it. If it's not a quizzical sort of eyebrow raise but rather an instinctive quick one and it goes in tandem with a smile, it means he thinks you—or whatever you are saying—are interesting.

On the other hand, a single raised eyebrow is a well-known sign of skepticism or displeasure. It has been referred to before as "the eyebrow cock." It's up to you to put things into context to decide exactly what this gesture means.

Is he Squirming or Fidgeting?

This is a reliable sign that something is wrong. He doesn't want to be right where he is now. He wants out. If he does this, things might not be looking good for the two of you.

You can think about this with yourself in mind as well. It's very common to squirm when you're uncomfortable. Even children do it. Squirming and fidgeting are slightly different. We're more concerned with the squirm. However, be considerate of what idea you might be projecting, and if he does both, that's just not a good sign.

The Eyes are the Window to the Soul

Here are a few clues you can read just from a person's eyes:

Is he looking into your eyes, letting his gaze linger longer than necessary? This is a good sign that he's interested in you or attracted to you. He wants to stare into your eyes for as long as he can.

If a person is trying to remember a sound or a particular set of sounds like a song, their eyes are likely to move directly to the left.

If a person is trying to recall an image, their eyes will move upwards and to the left.

A person trying to "see" a new picture or image will have their eyes go up and to the right.

Eyes that are tilted downward and to the left indicate that the person is mentally "talking to themselves."

These movements of the eye can apply directly to your ability to "read someone." If you ask a question and his eyes move up and to the left, he's genuinely trying to recall the correct answer so you can rest assured he doesn't intend to deceive you.

Lying

There are people who simply aren't so savory and then there exists in the world people of a truly Dark Psychosocial nature.

Let's talking about lying.

Ninety-one percent of people lie. It almost makes you wonder— could that be accurate? This is an estimate and I don't believe that anyone can truly know for sure. However, when we consider every single white lie and the not-so-white lies, maybe it's not so far-fetched.

For instance, how many sorts of "fibs" do those of us with children hear from them every day? They seem harmless and, in my opinion, most of them are.

How many times have you been getting ready to go out with a friend? She faces you and asks you, "How do I look? How do you like my dress? Do you like my hair?" What if you don't like her dress and her hair is awful? Oh, it sounds terrible, but we've all been there at one point or another.

Yet still, what are we to do? What would almost anyone do? Well, almost anyone would lie. It sounds so innocuous, such a harmless little "fib," and yet, it is a lie.

What about those times you go shopping with the girls? Do you bring in your take in plain sight of your husband? If he happens to count what you spent, do you embellish or do you say the straight truth?

How about with our children? What if he or she plays the cello and it sounds like nails on a chalkboard? Would you tell her that? Not likely. We want to encourage our children and instill confidence in that them. Most of us understand that one of those most important things in life is good self-esteem and confidence in our own abilities.

Most people are going to encourage that little boy or girl and tell them they're great whenever they need to hear it, regardless of whether or not we feel like listening to one more performance.

Considering just these things, is it bad to lie? I don't believe there is a black and white answer to that question. There is a definitive grey area.

There is a gigantic difference between cheating on your wife and telling her she looks beautiful in her red dress as you get ready for dinner, even if you wish she would have chosen the black one.

How much do they lie?

So, returning to body language. Are you single and hoping to meet a companion? What are the red flags? What sorts of bad body language signals speak louder than words can? As it turns out, there's many.

1. Dishonesty

As a child, I remember the distinct feeling that would happen when my parents were mad at me, when I would just cover my eyes. Up to a certain age, I actually thought that by covering my eyes so I don't see them, they could conversely not see me either. Sometimes, I would cover my eyes during a scary show. As we grow up, our realities grow different. We learn that just because we cover our eyes, the reality behind our eyes cannot be fully eradicated, and people can certainly still see us.

Just as these gestures change as we grow up, so do the more distinguished and "grown-up" signs of body language.

Very often, when we lie, we reflexively cover our mouth afterward. This is hardwired into our brains. We unconsciously cover our mouth after lying or being deceitful, as our brains unconsciously send signals to block what we consciously know is not true. However, the gestures that imply this are not obvious. Sometimes just rubbing the mouth or a fist— sometimes even a "fake" cough—can be overt signals. If you are a man or a woman trying to evaluate a potential partner, it's important that you watch for the subtle and not so subtle signals, especially if you feel interested in the person.

Going back again to that silly notion that most of us had as children where if we covered our eyes no one could see us, sometimes adults will actually rub their eyes instead. One would particularly close both their eyes but rub only one of them. It's somewhat of a two-fold attempt: cover up the lie with one eye, look the person in the eye with another. Avoiding eye contact altogether is a huge red flag. Liars can do it, but the most insidious among them know that you know this, so they deliberately cover one eye. It is rather cunning. It is not to be ignored.

2. Doubt and Uncertainty

Is this next one evil? That's for you to decide. We all experience that doubt. Uncertainty as well is inherent at times within all of us.

Purportedly, the body language for these feelings is to take a finger and scratch the earlobe or the neck a few times. This may be an ambiguous piece of body language. This could mean that this person is attempting to try to convey that they agree with you while in reality they actually doubt you.

3. Hot Under the Collar

This old phrase has been around forever—and for good reason. It generally signifies anger. Physical symptoms of anger have been known to cause actual flushing or itching on our necks. Scratching or tugging at our collars is indicative of a way to try to relieve that feeling. If you're interacting with someone and they knew this, especially if their neck turns red, you have an anger situation on your hands. Don't take this lightly. Anger is ugly and hard to cope with. The occasional one-off is one thing, but people who deal with a lot of anger can get very difficult very fast. It's quite ugly and frightening. Excessive anger can make a relationship incredibly complicated and difficult.

4. A Face that Lacks Emotion as You Speak

You're telling him an animated story, you turn to gauge his reaction, and it's blank. This is a sign that he's not into you. Seriously, there's not much point in wasting any more time on this one.

5. Fake Smile versus a Real Smile

The majority of us go about our days smiling. We smile at our colleagues or classmates, at the mail carrier, at the clerk behind the counter, and so on. A smile is a sweet gesture of good will.

However, it's easy to fake a smile too. We've all done it from time to time. Here's how you can tell the difference between a fake smile and a real one: a fake smile will involve the lip and the muscles around them. A genuine smile uses many more muscles in the face. It causes the cheekbones to rise and the skin around the eyes to crinkle.

Here's another simple way to tell: Real smiles pervade our eyes in a way that is virtually unmistakable. A genuine smile truly does "light up the eyes."

6. In a Hurry to Make an Exit

If a person is attracted to you, he's going to be comfortable to sit and chat for a bit. In fact, chances are he's not going to want to leave at all. If you're speaking with someone and they begin to give cues like looking at their watch more times than necessary or making sidelong glances at the exit, unless his time is absolutely needed elsewhere, a guy stepping away and trying to make a quick escape probably isn't attracted to you.

7. His Relationship with His Nose

It sounds odd, doesn't it? Many of us touch our nose for one reason or another during the conversation. The most classic one: it itches.

However, if a person seems to have a preoccupation with touching his nose—to an excessive extent—it's a good sign he doesn't care for you and it could signify that he's lying. Ouch. Neither situation is good so you may want to cross this one off your list.

8. His Toes

Well, perhaps not necessarily his toes, but in the way he's pointing them. The "wider" and more open a person is, the more chance that he's interested. However, say you're in close quarters and he can't sprawl on out on a sofa, get comfortable, and spread his legs out. Say you're standing in a line or a crowd instead. Look down at the direction in wish he's pointing his feet? Are they pointed at you or turned toward you? If they are, it is a good sign and indicates attraction.

9. Tired or Bored?

This one is kind of a no-brainer. We all get tired, but is it 4 p.m. or 4 a.m.? If a person can't stop yawning around you, it's probably because—quite simply—you bore him.

10. Proximity

You go to an outdoor market. Does he wander off every time you turn around? Does it seem like he's not there? Alternatively, is he constantly by your side the whole time? A man who is very attracted to you will be right up in your space. This one is easy to discern.

Many little gestures such as these will show he feels protective over you. If he does none of them and you are pretty much on your own, it is not a good sign.

Chapter 5:

How to Analyze Some of the Darker Traits in People

You will encounter people who will try to manipulate your psychology. Obviously, you would want to stay away from them. Like modern-day vampires, these people—if you let them—will exercise tactics to exploit you emotionally and suck you dry. They are very good at what they do and they benefit from the control they gain over you when they do this. These people prey on the weak. Therefore, it's your responsibility to make yourself strong.

Many people in our lives are the opposite and exhibit healthy mental influences. This is part of a good, healthy relationship, and it occurs more than sick ones. In healthy relationships, the parties do not victimize one another. There are no striking imbalances of power. One person isn't out for everything they can gain. Healthy relationships are a give-and-take situation. Neither party could be considered a victim.

I have listed fourteen ways in which people will try to gain control over others. This is not meant to be an exhaustive list, but rather a compilation of subtle as well as strident examples of coercion. Not everyone who acts in the following manners may be deliberately trying to manipulate you. Some people simply have very poor habits. Regardless, it's important to recognize these behaviors in situations where your rights, interests, and safety are at stake.

Conditional Love

A person should never say, "If you do this I'll love you." Real love does not come with a set of conditions. To tell someone you won't do something unless he or she does X, Y, or Z is manipulative and evil. A person who does this will try to make you feel guilty. Don't let anyone confuse you and think you've done anything wrong simply because you don't agree with what he or she wants you to do.

The Advantage of Being on Home Court

An individual who is out to manipulate and/or control you will want to meet you in what he or she considers his home turf. Having you be unfamiliar with your surroundings gives him an edge. It's better in these types of situations—whether it's a new encounter or even when there are problems to be dealt with—to meet in a neutral location.

Sitting Back and Letting You Do the Talking (at first)

Have you ever noticed how a salesperson will try to work you by letting you do all the talking at first? They have a set of seemingly casual questions that they'll ask you deliberately to discover the things in your armor. Once they have done this, they swoop in from their side and start chipping away at you. They will use the information they have gleaned to put you on the spot or right where they want you so they can make the sale before you know what hit you.

Arm yourself with the ability to tell the difference between a person like the one above and someone who just really likes to chat. If you use your instincts, you should know soon enough.

Twisting the Facts

This is when someone lies and blames you and plays the victim card when you are the real victim. There will be people who will do this for one reason or another. Sometimes it's simply because they feel guilty. Regardless, it's not okay and is a bad sign. The only way a successful relationship can happen between two people is when they are both_honest. Lying to make themselves look better and you worse is particularly spiteful and a sign that this person does not care for you as much as they should. It's a sign of a lack of character.

Restricting Your Actions with Others

When he tries to limit whom you will see, talk to, or interact with, he's doing this for a reason. It's a way for him to control your social life by telling you what is and isn't okay with whom—and when. This is extremely unhealthy. Healthy couples trust each other enough to let them have their own set of friends and spend time with them when they wish to because when they are feeling the security of trust, there is no need to control.

Raising Their Voice and Displaying Negative Emotions

Some individuals raise their voice during discussions as a form of aggressive manipulation. The assumption may be that if they project their voice loudly enough or display negative emotions, you'll submit to their coercion and give them what they want. The aggressive voice is frequently combined with strong gestures to increase impact. This is a sign that this person is carrying around too much anger that they aren't properly dealing with. Yelling is mean and intimidating to others and is a childish attempt to get one's way.

Confusing You with Too Much Information

Some people want to break you down by making you believe they are so much smarter than you are. They might do this by inundating you with facts in a field in which they know you aren't well versed. This can be done in many different ways, but the bottom line is they have a better chance of bending you to their will if they can establish their intellectual superiority towards you. Keep in mind that this is different from an actual smart person. The problem happens when they try to make you feel that you are less of a person because they have expertise in areas that you don't.

Negative Surprises

Some people use negative surprises to put you off balance and gain a psychological advantage. This can range from low-balling in a negotiation situation to a sudden promise that they will not be able to come through and deliver in some way. Typically, the unexpected negative information comes without warning, so you have little time to prepare and counter their move. The manipulator may ask for additional concessions from you in order to continue working with you.

Giving You Little or No Time to Decide

This is a common trick used in sales; the "con-artist" applies pressure on you to make a decision before you're ready. By creating a sense of urgency and an atmosphere of tension, they gain control over you. The entire point, of course, is to cave and give in to the aggressor's demands.

Targeting Your Weaknesses with Negative Humor

I have witnessed unhealthy relationships where the man was consistently critical of the woman. The way she dressed and presented herself was never good enough. Dinners were criticized, and so on. This can break a person's spirit down very rapidly. Some manipulators like to make critical remarks but disguise them as humor to make you seem inferior and less secure. Examples can include any variety of comments ranging from your clothing ensemble to your educational background, the kind of car you drive, or that you were five minutes late to dinner with friends. It may not seem blatantly so, but this kind of behavior is nothing short of abuse, and being exposed to it for too long has much potential to break your spirit down.

Red Tape

Have you come into the unfortunate situation of having to face bankruptcy or divorce? For what it's worth, don't let yourself be talked into doing it without hiring a lawyer. You owe it to yourself to have your own back. This person knows all your weaknesses, and unless you know that they are of good character, keep yourself protected. Sadly, by this point in the relationship, they're going to be looking out for number 1— obviously, that's not you.

Chipping Away at Your Self-Esteem

This is different from the humorous jabs here and there; this is when you are being outright abused. Your confidence is being eroded each time this person chooses a topic and goes off about it. You must not allow yourself to be ridiculed. Between the humorous jabs and the jabs at your self-esteem, your confidence is being destroyed. You cannot win with a Dark Personality. The only way through and up is out. Cut your losses as early as you can. Learn from the mistake and move on.

Putting You in the Backburner

You call repeatedly but receive no answer. You notice that when he is home and his phone rings he picks it up by the third ring. He is quiet and will not speak to you. He's attempting to gain more control by giving you the silent treatment. This is going to make you feel terrible if you let it. Alternatively, you can recognize that he is a dark person and that he's not meant for you because someone that is would never treat you this way. Internalize this truth.

Feigning Ignorance

Children do this. It's actually quite humorous. They think that if you can't make them understand what it is you want from them, they can get out of doing it. Does he pretend he doesn't know what you're talking about when you are sure that he does? Does he forget important things? Has he ruined evenings out and such this way? This is his way of (1) keeping you thrown off base and (2) getting out of anything he doesn't want to have to do while pleading innocence. This is the classic "playing dumb" tactic. This is master manipulator stuff. Only someone who with truly dark intentions is capable of treating another human being this way. This person is not for you. Even if it's hard to go, *go*. There is so much better out there for you.

Guilt Baiting

Here are some examples: Unreasonable blaming, targeting the recipient's soft spot, and holding another responsible for the manipulator's happiness and success or unhappiness and failures.

By targeting the recipient's emotional weaknesses and vulnerability, the manipulator coerces the recipient into ceding unreasonable requests and demands.

Hitting You with Red Tape

This often happens in divorce and is the reason why you should never go through a divorce with someone unless you are very amicable and you know you can trust the person. There's not only a lot of paperwork but also, these days, there are more obscure laws than ever, and they vary from state to state.

Victimhood

Repeatedly heaping negativity on someone will make him or her feel bad like a victim when actually he or she is not. The reason is that the manipulator easily gains power over a broken-down, victim-like person.

Attempting to Manipulate Your Emotions

Some partners will try to make the other feel anxious and guilty. They knew if they can get you to doubt yourself and get your emotions all twisted up, you will be easier to control. Some people truly are master manipulators.

Trust Issues

If you haven't given them any apparent reason not to trust you but they still don't, it is a big red flag. People who cannot inherently trust other people are disturbed on some level and they would benefit from some kind of professional help.

If he is going through your things, trying to listen in on your calls or read your messages, or quizzing you incessantly on your whereabouts, this could signify a major problem between the two of you.

Hostility in their Actions toward You

Hostility of any kind means you should leave the relationship as fast as you can and do not look back. It doesn't matter whether you are threatened or not, and it's even more reason to leave when it becomes violent.

Rarely do violent people ever change for good. It is a terrible situation and no one should have to live that way. Don't let that happen to you.

The Relationship Simply Doesn't Feel Right

Do you get unpleasant butterflies in your stomach when he walks through the door? Are you feeling drained a lot of time? Does the person you're with make you nervous?

Our brains and nervous systems are incredible tools when it comes to catching whether or not we're at the right place at the right time—in other words, a healthy situation. If you are feeling contradicting signals, pay close attention to them.

This one ties right in with self-esteem. We all want to feel high self-esteem and feel good about ourselves. If you feel like your self-esteem is dragging, sit down at the table and take note of all of the things going on in your life. If a person or a relationship is the affecting your self-esteem in a negative way, it's advisable to consider leaving that relationship as soon as possible.

I hope you've been able to get at least an early grasp on body language and reading personalities. There is much about it on the internet and many more books if you decide you want to go more in depth.

Chapter 6:

Personality Types

What would a world be like wherein we can simply read what other people are feeling all the time? What if people walked constantly displaying "thought-bubbles" like characters in a comic book?

In my opinion, that would make life much too easy and a bit boring. Getting to know people is a great joy. Think about the last time you met a person who turned out to be a very good friend. Do you remember your early interactions—those times when you didn't really have any idea what that person was thinking? Perhaps you felt a little nervous around them because you did not want to say the wrong thing, and because of this, you proverbially stuck your foot in your mouth.

No, I don't believe our world would be as interesting if every bit of the guesswork was taken out of our interactions with other people. The "getting to know someone" is a dance that has been playing out since the beginning of time. It's a rather lovely dance...

...except when it's not!

Having said that, I can think of many instances in my life where I would have been saved a lot of grief I could have cut to the chase with another human being and known what they were about instantly. It's likely that everyone reading this will be able to bring to mind a similar instance in his or her lives.

There are a million types of people in the world. Being an optimist, I believe that while we all make mistakes of different magnitudes—some of them huge—underneath it all, the human race is essentially "good." However, that doesn't mean that there aren't many bad people in existence as well—dark people if you will. You cannot trust these people in one way or the other. You do not want these people in your life. There are even plenty of dangerous people. To bring up a very old adage, the world has excessively many "wolves in sheep's clothing."

While we don't exactly have the ability to read minds yet, I believe the time is coming. Some of you may feel like that is extremely farfetched. Because of the era I have grown up in and the mind-blowingly incredible leaps and bounds I have seen play out scientifically, I've truly had it ingrained in me that anything is possible. I clearly remember the controversy over whether or not we could ever put a human being on the moon, and yet we put Neil Armstrong there.

Now, I'm living in a time where companies exist solely for creating livable conditions on Mars and designing transportation to get there of which the average human could eventually afford to take advantage. Again, dear readers, I truly believe that anything is possible.

In reality, there are too many reasons to list about why it's a good idea to learn to "read" our fellow human beings to whatever degree it would be possible. Fortunately, it is possible to an extent and then some if it's something you find yourself fascinated with genuinely. Not only is it fascinating, but imagine the usefulness, especially when it comes to the most important things we do such us rearing our own children and choosing our life partners, not to mention friends and employers (or employees).

One thing about people—all of us are complicated and multi-layered. Few people could be categorized as simple. As a result, when you delve into the study and analysis and the act of trying to "read" people, you're taking on a chunk of learning and studying. The more effort you put into it, though, like anything else, the more rewards you reap.

The clues are as incredibly simple as words are said and the mannerisms exhibited when they are. Full on eye contact, the lack thereof, or all of the varying degrees are a huge part of the portal into the inner workings of another person's mind.

Most people seem real, and most people are—on the surface. However, there are many layers between the surface and the core, and our job is to learn to read those layers in order to understand the core.

One of the beauties of being able to "read" what is really going on with people is that you can actually do really amazing, important things with a skill like that. There's nothing wrong with wanting to benefit yourself by honing these skills, and yet, how many people do you think each one of us could help out of serious trouble if we truly knew how to read where a person's heart, mind, and soul are?

Millions of people suffer from a mental illness of some form. Many of these people don't reach out for help because they are overwhelmed and they honestly aren't sure how to go about it. It's very common among mentally ill people, and when I say mentally ill, I'm talking about people who suffer from depression, anxiety disorders, bipolar disorders, schizophrenia, and so on. Then, of course, there is a whole spectrum of autistic disorders. The simple, heartbreaking fact is that so many of these people walk through life dealing with this alone. The truth is that they don't have anyone in their lives who truly understand them, and they have neither the courage nor the strength to make themselves understood. It's truly awful. I can't imagine the loneliness and pain inherent in an existence where you aren't (or truly believe you aren't) understood by another human. So there it is: learning to read people isn't something simply there to benefit us. It's there for a higher good as well.

The very first step in learning to analyze personality types in other people is to become well versed in your own. Nothing but good can come from knowing yourself. In fact, if you examine your life through hindsight, chances are that you would have made many choices differently if you had understood yourself better. It sounds strange, but not everyone knows himself or herself and some people just go through life committing serial blunders with very few good results. There's an old saying that goes: "Insanity is committing the same mistakes over and over and expecting different results." Does it sound familiar at all? Why does this happen? I believe it happens because we don't know ourselves as well as we should. It's all right, though. It's never too late to turn that (or anything else) around.

By working on learning to analyze people, you become a great asset to your friends and family because suddenly you are the one who seems to have the most empathy. Being able to empathize with people is perhaps the greatest gift you can give them along with being a good listener. Your studies in analyzing people will vastly improve both.

"Each person seems to be energized more by either the external world (extraversion) or the internal world (introversion)." —Carl Jung

In my research for this book, I came across a work by Carl Jung. Jung is an incredibly influential Psychiatrist and Psychotherapist who lived in the early 20s. At first, he was a disciple of Sigmund Freud, the incredibly popular influential Psychiatrist. At some point, Jung began to break off and form some of his own ideas. The comparisons and contrasts between their two ideologies are incredible and certainly worth reading about as you study Psychiatry and Psychology.

The work that I am referring to, in particular, is called "Psychological Types." It's a very fascinating read, but to break it down to the essentials, Jung categorized personality types into one of the following four plus "introverted" and "extroverted."

- Sensing
- Intuiting
- Thinking
- Functioning

He actually devised an incredibly complicated construct, which still stands on its own in Psychiatry circles to this day. In this theory, he also incorporates the idea of the introverted personality and the extroverted personality. His line of thinking explains that each one of the various personality types experiences the world in very different ways. The way he referenced this was to use the first letters of those two words (extroverted and introverted) in lower case and then pair them next to the main construct. For example, "Se" would mean "Sensing extrovert,) and so on.

I'll touch on theories without going too much into depth because there is so much more to be said here, and it's my hope that this topic will fascinate you enough that you'll be seeking out the literature yourself.

To give you an example, I'll expound on these personality types as Jung saw them, although these can only be considered a "synopsis" as there is much more to learn.

Perhaps you are aware of the "Mindfulness" and "Mindfulness Meditation" movement that has had a huge resurgence recently. The premise of Mindfulness, most simply put, is learning to live in the moment. In other words, people who practice Mindfulness don't dwell on the past or worry about the future. To them, life is simply a series of one moment after another, and the goal is to live each as fully as possible. The construct behind this is that too many of us "waste" too much or our lives dwelling on what has already happened or worrying about a future that we don't know is even going to happen. Life is short and we truly never have any way of knowing when our number will come up, so other than some basic common sense planning and worrying, dwelling on what may be ahead is a perfect waste of time. I don't know about you, but if I'm going to waste time, I can think of more fun ways to do it!

Extroverted Sensing (Se)

An *Se* type is about what there to offer at the moment: sights, sounds, smells, and sensations. They welcome new experiences and want to spend each one "at the moment."

These are all wonderful qualities and yet according to Jung, these types of people need to expand their horizons. They do need to look at planning the future in a more serious way. They have a hard time accepting that they can't just "jump into" the experience of every moment, even sometimes to the detriment of things that actually need to be done—you know, practical real-life sorts of things. These types of people are the ones one might say walk around with their head a bit "in the clouds."

Introverted Sensing (Si)

These folks are not impulsive. In fact, they are hard workers who are rooted in tradition. They need to be given time to think before they decide to embrace new concepts. This person does not decide that he needs a new car and buys it in the same way.

The best thing you can do for a personality of this type is to recognize their nature and their propensity to "weigh" everything out and think things over. Time and patience are what these people need. You're getting almost the opposite of impulsive. Support them with understanding and patience.

Introverted Intuition (Ni)

Again, because of this introverted side, these people spend a significant amount of their productive time alone. They lean towards putting together how things work by working through the process of analyzing things internally. They aren't as interested in "facts" as they are in the reasons why the facts came together. They trust their gut feeling more than what is going on outside of themselves. They need time to be allowed to come up with exactly what it is they want to do. Once they do, look out. They are good at learning from experiences in order not to repeat mistakes. These are generally brilliant people.

Extroverted Intuition (Ne)

This personality type thrives on external stimuli. They might be that person you know who seems "all over the place." With these people, we want to allow them to be sidetracked as they need to. However, as a friend, gently help guide them back onto the path and definitely appreciate the great sense of humor they have. Don't let the fact that they can be a little flighty fool you into thinking they are not smart because they generally are. These people have creative minds and they often make excellent leaders.

Extroverted Thinking (Te)

These smart intelligent people conserve the energy within their minds and put it to the highest purposes. For these people, logic rules. They are getting at lining up how to get from A-to-Z in the most straightforward way. They're visual and like to rely on props (think Math Professor). They take everything in and consider all possibilities prior to making decisions.

If you're a woman married to a man like this and you go to him with a problem, don't expect a hug; expect a solution. This is a very pragmatic personality type. They can almost seem cold sometimes because of their reliance upon logic compared to feelings.

Introverted Thinking (Ti)

The thinking and reasoning of these people do not necessarily rely on external props. This makes for a more profound decision-making process. They do want to know how things work, though. Give them a car a computer to take apart and put back together. If what you're doing is not productive, don't expect this friend to take too much interest.

They are best off given some space because even though they might have a tendency to go awry in their thinking in the beginning, they will "self-correct." The reason for this is their need to understand the topic completely before they're satisfied. These types can get easily overwhelmed by too many emotional stimuli so they may require some extra help in that area.

Extroverted Feeling (Fe)

These are people that as you talk to, they'll be considering your words, but you might not realize it because they might not give that many cues. These personality types choose their friends discriminately because they are generally very moralistic and upstanding. A friend of this type will be very empathetic and notice your mood. If it's not a good mood, they'll help you solve it. They're good at that type of thing, not just with one person but also in groups.

These people are good people to be friends with. They are incredibly supportive and, unlike someone who is much more pragmatic all the time, they are able to exhibit more nurturing qualities. These types usually have many close friends.

Introverted Feeling (Fi)

These people are on a quest to know exactly who they are and to know their place in the world. It's a very dominant trait. These people see things in black and white, and also good and bad. They can sometimes struggle with the grey area. Many of them care very much about their environment and their surroundings and have desires and ambitions to make the world a better place somehow.

This type of people forms instantaneous bonds or fall in love at first sight, and yet they do form very close bonds once they get there. They are loyal almost to a fault.

There are many different constructs of personality types—probably just as many as there are personalities to read. This one by Jung has stood the test of time. Likely hundreds of books are out there discussing it so I encourage you to study it further if it fascinates you and you feel like zooming in on people with these "types" in mind helps you to understand them better.

Chapter 7:

Dark Psychology

We are so naive that we don't know that there are some very dark individuals in the world. Murderers, thieves, abusers, the list could go on.

No one wants to be friends or be associated with these types of people, yet there are people in the world that are pretty dark, even if they don't do any of the above-mentioned things.

Unfortunately, there exist in the world people who are like vampires. They would suck the life out of you if you let them. There are people who would walk all over you to make it one more step up the ladder, without looking twice.

At the heart of Dark Psychology is something called Covert Emotional Manipulation. An article in <u>Psychology Today</u> defines it like this: "Psychological manipulation can be defined as the exercise of undue influence through mental distortion and emotional exploitation with the intention to seize power, control, benefits, and/or privileges at the victim's expense."

Covert simply means the victim is unaware that they are being preyed upon. To this end, and for their own gains, people work against you and your emotions, your beliefs, your behaviors and more.

There are many Dark Psychology Types in this world, and we must keep an eye on much of them. Here are four of the most prominent in modern studies:

The Narcissist

According to Psychology Today, the following is the definition of a Narcissist:

"The hallmarks of Narcissistic Personality Disorder (NPD) are grandiosity, a lack of empathy for other people, and a need for admiration. People with this condition are frequently described as arrogant, self-centered, manipulative, and demanding."

The bottom line is that narcissists have an incredibly inflated view of themselves, and they absolutely must feel admired up to the point where it is near worship or they cannot be happy otherwise. Some of the greatest entertainers in the world have been said to be Narcissists. It is easy to see why.

When you spot one, it's best to keep as much distance as you can. No good can come out of a relationship with a true narcissist.

Machiavellians

This is a type of psychopathic personality, and we all know this isn't good. These folks differ from a narcissist in a way that they all seemed to have earned a degree in manipulation from the top "Dark University" in the world. If there could be said such a thing, a Machiavellian has been called a more "socially acceptable" version of a psychopath. Their darkest quality is to the degree that they can manipulate others to their own selfish degrees and yet feel no guilt from it.

Psychopaths

Psychopaths are truly frightening people. From a very early age in their lives, they can commit acts of atrocity and feel no guilt.

These people can live a kind of "anything goes" scenario, and most of them do. To name just of few of their despicable qualities, they are usually grandiose, incredibly callous, and dastardly manipulative. True psychopaths are capable of violence and even murder. You never want to associate yourself with these kinds of people.

Sadists

Sadists may not score as high on the scale of manipulative-ness as the other Dark Psychology types listed here, but one thing sets them apart from the others. Sadists get off on cruelty—and I mean they *really* get off on it. Because they like to put themselves into positions where they can get away with it as often as possible, many of them are police officers, which is a horrifying thought.

Del Palhouse has been studying Dark Psychology for a number of years. He finds these people more interesting than good, happy people. In a way, I see his point. These people are truly fascinating, to a point, but to me, they are as fascinating as the stars of superbly written Hollywood screenplays.

However, these are frightening people. I would never want myself, my daughter, or anyone I care about to associate with these people.

I think that is the biggest reason why it is our responsibility to study these people: so that we have the ability to recognize them when we see them, then turn and run the other way as quickly as we can. In this admiration, good or bad, and the case of a narcissist, it's rarely good.

Between regular psychology and the study of personality types, getting to know what various body signals mean, looking at personality types and delving into "Dark Psychology," it is my hope that this book has given you some basic knowledge, plenty of things to think about, and thoughts about which areas you may go to delve into deeper. There is absolutely no shortage of books on these topics.

Conclusion

Thank you for making it through to the end of *How to Analyze People Techniques for Reading Body Language and Identifying Personality Types and Dark Psychology*. I hope you thoroughly enjoyed it.

My wish for you is that it was what you wanted it to be, that it touched on the subjects you are most fascinated with, and that it has piqued your interest in the further study of these topics— each of which could fill a whole book and many more.

I hope you have been given a grasp of the most basic of body language, like what it means when you're standing next to someone and his or her toes are pointed outward. In my research for this book, I discovered all kinds of things like that I would never have thought of in a million years.

I hope it's easier you to judge a closed-off person from a more open one and that if you are looking for friends or a mate, you have a better idea now of what to look for.

Please remember that the Jungian personality types were just one construct (albeit a much respected and popular one) in that area and that there are many more where those came from if you are interested in more of that sort of knowledge.

My biggest wish is that you learned something you didn't know and had an enjoyable read while doing it.

I wish the best of luck to you in your quest to learn and in your endeavors, whatever they may be.

41686536R00033

Printed in Poland
by Amazon Fulfillment
Poland Sp. z o.o., Wrocław